Foods for All Seasons

Recipes and photographs by
Béla Liscsinszky

Foods
for All Seasons

AUTUMN

in the Golden Dragon Inn

Corvina

A special note of thanks:
The writing of *Foods for All Seasons* would not have been possible without the assistance of my colleague, chef Csaba Németh. I also wish to record my debt to photographer Tamás Urbán and to János Krajcsovics, who so generously lent me tableware from his former antique store in Szentendre. And last but not least I would like to express my gratitude to Attila Máhr, owner of the Golden Dragon Restaurant, for his encouragement and support.
The recipes in this book serve **four** persons.
Metric weights and measures are followed by American cup measures. One American cup = 8 fluid ounces; one American pint = 2 cups; one American quart = 32 fluid ounces = 4 cups.

Béla Liscsinszky

Recipes

Coddled quail's eggs

(a hot supper dish)

Ingredients

20 quail's eggs
200 ml/1 cup cream
1 red-skinned onion
200 g/7 oz cottage cheese
80 g/3 oz butter
1 bunch chives
2 tbsp sour cream
salt, nutmeg

To prepare

Rub the cottage cheese through
a sieve and blend until smooth
with 50 g (¼ cup) butter, salt
and the sour cream.
Finely chop the onion and the
chives and season with a dash
of salt.

To cook

Beat the quail's eggs with
a dash of salt, grated nutmeg
and cream. The mixture should
not become frothy. Pour into
cups lightly greased with butter.
Place the cups in a pan which
contains 5 cm (2 in) of water.
Half-cover the pan and simmer
over a very low heat for about
30 minutes. Meanwhile toast the
bread, spread with butter and
creamed cottage cheese and
sprinkle with onion and chives.
When the mixture is firm, serve
hot with the freshly made toast.

Mushroom consommé

Ingredients

400 g/14 oz mushrooms
300 g/10 oz beef bones
100 g/4 oz carrots
100 g/4 oz parsnips
50 g/1 small onion
2 bunches parsley
1 white of egg
½ tsp tomato paste, salt
peppercorn
20 g/1 tbsp butter
2 cloves garlic
200 ml/1 cup red wine

To prepare

Trim and wipe the mushrooms
and reserve the four finest and
whitest mushroom caps. Finely
chop the rest.
Trim and slice the carrots and
parsnips, finely chop the onion
and the parsley.

To cook

Beat the white of egg until semi-
stiff, fold in a little tomato paste,
then combine with the finely
chopped mushrooms and parsley. Add 1 ½ litres (3 pints) cold
water and the red wine. Add to
this mixture the bones and
vegetables and season with salt,
pepper and garlic. Cook over
a low heat for about 1 hour.
Strain through a fine sieve. Just
before serving, thinly slice the
reserved mushroom caps, sauté
them in a little butter and add to
the piping hot mushroom con-
sommé.

Lux salad

Ingredients

300 g/10 oz chestnuts
150 g/5 oz beets
400 g/14 oz apples
200 g/7 oz celeriac
1 head lettuce
40 g/1 small onion, sliced
salt, peppercorns, sugar
vinegar, caraway seed
200 ml/1 cup yogurt
100 ml/½ cup cooking oil
dry white wine (optional)

To prepare

Score each chestnut and bake in a hot oven.
Sprinkle a little water over them before removing from the oven to facilitate shelling. Using a sharp knife, finely chop the shelled chestnuts. Wash and pare the celeriac. Slice and cobble them, then flavour with a dash of salt, peppercorns, sugar, vinegar and onion. Chill, then drain. Wash the beets, sprinkle with caraway seeds and cook until tender. Chill and pare. Put into a blender with the yogurt, and cooking oil. Season with salt, sugar, vinegar and thin if necessary with white wine.
Wash the lettuce and separate the leaves. Carefully combine the lettuce leaves, the pared and sliced apple, celeriac and the chestnuts with the beet-yogurt dressing. Serve thoroughly chilled.

13

Ingredients

4 (800–900 g/1¾–2 lb) legs of goose
300 g/10 oz leeks
100 g/4 oz canned pearl onions
2 cloves garlic, 1 bunch parsley
300 g/10 oz pimientos
250 g/8–9 oz canned green beans
salt, ground black pepper
1 tbsp lard, marjoram

To prepare

Salt the legs of goose and rub them with marjoram. Lard them with garlic, sprinkle with melted butter and roast in a moderate oven. Do not put water in the roasting pan, but baste the roast with its own fat. When the meat has browned but is still uncooked, cover with aluminium foil and continue roasting for about 1 hour.

To cook

Clean the leeks thoroughly and slice them into rings. Pour the pan juices into a skillet and sauté the leek rings in this. Stir in the drained canned pearl onions, sliced pimientos, and the finely chopped parsley. A few minutes later add the drained green beans and, after another few minutes, mound this ragout on top of the roast legs of goose.

15

Stuffed pork chops

1. Heap the filling over half the flattened chops...
2. Cover them with the other half...
3. Secure edges with a skewer, and dip in breadcrumbs mixed with cheese

Ingredients

8 (800 g/1¾ lb) pork chops
5 eggs, 80 g/3 oz flour
100 g/4 oz breadcrumbs
1 bunch parsley
100 g/4 oz grated cheese
600 g/1¼ lb Brussels sprouts
½ l/2¼ cups cooking oil
or lard for the frying
salt, ground black pepper
50 g/2 oz butter

To prepare

The filling: Boil 2 eggs for 10 minutes. Cool, remove the shells and finely chop the eggs. Combine with finely chopped parsley, 50 g (2 oz) grated cheese and 1 raw egg. Season with salt and pepper.
Trim the Brussels sprouts and boil them in salted water. Toss in hot butter before serving.

To cook

Slightly flatten the pork chops, and dip both sides into seasoned flour. Arrange the filling over four slices of meat and cover them with the remaining four slices. Secure each with a skewer. Carefully dip the stuffed pork chops in beaten eggs and breadcrumbs into which you have mixed the rest of the cheese. Fry in hot cooking oil until brown. Serve with Brussels sprouts tossed in butter and tomato-onion ragout.
Tomato-onion ragout
Sauté 100 g (4 oz) finely chopped onion on 30 g (2 tbsp) lard. Add 200 ml (1 cup) ketchup and 100 ml (½ cup) red wine. Season with salt, lemon juice and ground black pepper, boil for a few minutes and serve immediately.

Ingredients

2 breasts of duck
20 g/2 tbsp lard
50 g/2 oz butter
salt, marjoram
1½ kg/3 lb winter squash
200 ml/1 cup dry white wine
ground nutmeg, grated lemon
rind

To prepare

Salt the meat and sprinkle it
with marjoram. Pare the squash,
remove centre and cut the flesh
into 1 cm (½ in) slices.

To cook

Place the breast of duck in a
lightly greased roasting pan and
roast in hot oven (180–200 °C/
375–400 °F). Baste frequently
with the fat which collects under
the meat. Bone the meat and
cut it into 2–3 cm (1 in) slices.
Serve with squash sautéed in
white wine and plums cooked in
wine (for the recipe of the latter,
see *Crispy roast pork,* p 43).
Sautéed squash: Fry both sides
of the squash slices in hot butter. Now add the white wine
and cook until tender. All the
juice must evaporate by the end
of cooking.
Season with ground nutmeg
and grated lemon rind.

Breast of duck with sautéed winter squash

Tripe with sauerkraut

Ingredients

600 g/1¼ lb tripe
200 g/7 oz smoked sausage
400 g/14 oz sauerkraut
150 g/3 small onions
50 g/3 slices smoked bacon
4 cloves garlic, 2 hot green
peppers
1 lemon, 1 tbsp paprika
200 ml/1 cup red wine

To prepare

Cut the tripe into slices 3–4 cm
(1–2 in) long and 2 cm (1 in)
wide. Turn briskly in salt and
lemon juice, leave to stand for
½ hour, then thoroughly wash
in plenty of water. Dice the
smoked bacon and slice the
onion thinly.

To cook

Render the bacon and sauté the
onion in its fat. Sprinkle with
paprika and stir it in quickly and
thin with 200 ml (1 cup) water.
Bring to the boil, add crushed
garlic and the prepared tripe.
Cook for about 1½–2 hours until
almost tender, stirring
frequently and replacing the
evaporated cooking liquor with
water. Then add the sauerkraut
and the chunks of sausage. Pour
in the red wine and cook until
tender. Season to taste with salt
and hot paprika. Serve with
a light red wine.

Shin of beef, Csongrád style

Ingredients

800 g/1¾ lb shin of beef
30 g/2 tbsp lard
20 g/2 tbsp paprika
2 cherry peppers
4 cloves garlic
200 ml/1 cup red wine
100 g/4 oz onion, chopped
salt

To prepare

Sear both sides of the meat in two-thirds of the hot lard, then set aside. Sauté the onion in the rest of the lard, sprinkle with paprika and thin with the red wine. Add sufficient water so that when the meat is replaced it will just be covered with cooking liquor. Season with crushed garlic, cherry peppers and salt and bring to the boil. Now replace the meat and cook, covered, over a low heat for about 1½ hours. Carve the meat before serving and strain the cooking liquor. Serve with cottage cheese dumplings.

Cottage cheese dumplings

Ingredients: 500 g/1 lb cottage cheese, 100 g/4 oz flour, 3 eggs, salt

Combine the cottage cheese with the eggs, salt and flour. Using a tablespoon, shape dumplings from this mixture and plunge them into boiling salted water. Leave the dumplings in the water until ready to serve.

Ingredients

500 g/18 oz flour, 160 g/5 oz lard
170 g/6 oz castor sugar
10 g/2 tsp baking powder
4 eggs
300 ml/1½ cups milk
300 g/10–11 oz castor sugar
100 ml/½ cup rum
50 g/2 oz raisins
100 g/4 oz ground walnuts
2 tbsp apricot jam
200 g/7 oz canned peaches
grated lemon rind

To prepare

Work the flour with the lard,
170 g (¾ cup) castor sugar, baking powder, 4 egg yolks and 100
ml (½ cup) milk. Divide into
three equal parts and roll out
each into an oblong 1 cm (½ in)
thick. Bake in a moderate
(170–190 °C/325–375 °F) oven.
When the pastry has cooled,
crumble one of the sheets and
work together with 200 ml
(1 cup) milk, 100 g (½ cup) castor sugar, the raisins, which
have been soaked in the rum,
the ground walnuts, the apricot
jam, the diced canned peaches
and the grated lemon rind. Use
this mixture as a filling to make
a sandwich with the remaining
two pastry sheets.
Beat the 4 whites of egg and
200 g (1 cup) castor sugar until
stiff over steam. Spread over the
top. Leave to stand in a dry
place for 1 day, then cut up into
squares.

Rum squares

Meat pâté

Ingredients

250 g/8–9 oz breast of turkey, boned
250 g/8–9 oz lean leg of pork
salt, black pepper, nutmeg
70 g/2½ oz butter
50 g/2 oz flour
200 ml/1 cup milk, 2 eggs
grated lemon rind

To prepare

Brown the flour in 50 g (4 tbsp) butter and add the boiling milk to it. Cook, stirring constantly, until the mixture comes off the side of the pan. Leave to cool in two equal parts. Finely grind one half with the turkey, the other half with the pork. Combine each mixture with a raw egg. Season the turkey with salt, pepper and nutmeg, the pork with salt, pepper and grated lemon rind.

To cook

Fill a buttered meat-loaf pan or an oven-proof dish with the pork mixture, smooth over the top, then top with the ground turkey. Smooth the surface with wet fingers and cover securely with aluminium foil.
Stand the dish in a baking pan half-filled with water and bake in a very slow oven (90 ℃/200 ° F) for 50 minutes.
Remove the foil, carefully turn the pâté out of the mold and serve piping hot. Meat pâté is also excellent served cold. However, in this case slightly press the meat pâté down before leaving it to cool. Garnish with various fresh or dried fruits.

Goose giblet soup

Ingredients

600 g/1¼ lb goose giblets
100 g/2 small onions
150 g/5 oz carrots
150 g/5 oz parsnips
50 g/2 oz celeriac
50 g/2 oz kohlrabi
4 cloves garlic, salt
peppercorn, allspice, marjoram
100 g/4 oz dry shell-shaped
pasta
200 g/7 oz fresh horseradish
3 tbsp vinegar, 1 tbsp sugar

To prepare

Trim the vegetables and cut into
wedges.
Pare and grate the horseradish.
Boil the pasta in salted water.

To cook

Wash the goose giblets and
bring to the boil in 1½ l (3 pints)
cold water. Skim and add the
prepared vegetables, onion and
garlic. Season with salt, pepper,
allspice and marjoram. Cook
over a low heat until the giblets
are tender. Strain through a fine
sieve, arrange cooked soup vegetables and giblets on a plate
and keep hot until served. Reheat the soup with the shell-
shaped pasta in it and serve
immediately. After finishing this
delicious soup the cooked soup
vegetables and the giblets
should be served separately
with pickled horseradish.

Pickled horseradish

Place the grated horseradish in
a tea strainer. Hold over steam
for 7 to 8 minutes, taking care
lest it touch the water. Horseradish steamed in this manner
loses its wildly bitter taste. Now
combine with salt, a little sugar,
vinegar and a few tablespoons
of water. Serve cold.

Beet salad with apples

Ingredients

300 g/¾ lb beets
200 g/½ lb apples, preferably Jonathan
1 lemon, 100 ml/½ cup olive oil
3 tbsp wine vinegar
salt, caraway seed
40 g/1 small onion, castor sugar

To prepare

Cook the beets in salted water flavoured with caraway seed and onion. Chill, pare and cut into thin strips. Pare the apples and also cut them into thin strips.
Carefully mix the beets, apples and lemon with the olive oil and the wine vinegar. Season with a dash of salt and sweeten with castor sugar according to taste. We recommend this dish as an accompaniment to breaded fish and meat.

Loin of pork with chestnuts

Ingredients

800 g/1¾ lb loin of pork
300 g/10 oz baked chestnuts, shelled
150 g/5 oz carrots
100 g/4 oz parsnips
50 g/2 oz celeriac
80 g/2 small onions
50 g/3 tbsp tomato paste
200 ml/1 cup red wine
200 ml/1 cup cream, 1 tsp flour
salt, granulated sugar, bay leaf
thyme
1 lemon, 30 g/2 tbsp lard
50 g/3 slices smoked bacon

To prepare

Bone the meat, season with salt and put the whole piece into a greased roasting pan. Roast in a hot oven for 40 to 45 minutes. Baste frequently with lard. Do not add water during cooking. When the meat is half done, cover it with aluminium foil. Cut the pared vegetables and the onion into slices of equal thickness. Leave half the shelled chestnuts in chunks, and grate the other half. Break the bone removed from the meat into pieces and roast, together with the pork, for 20 to 25 minutes. Do not add water.

To cook

Render the smoked bacon and caramelize 1 tsp sugar in its fat. Sauté the onion and the vegetables in the bacon fat, add the tomato paste and thin with red wine. Bring to the boil and add the roasted bones. Season with salt, bay leaf, and thyme and cook, in water to cover, over a low heat, for ½ hour. Remove the bones, and add the grated chestnuts. Boil for 10 minutes, then put the pan contents through a blender or rub through a sieve. Heat this mixture once again and add to it a smooth mixture of cream and flour. Season to taste with salt and lemon juice and add the chunks of chestnut. Heat once again and pour over the carved meat. Serve this dish with vegetable croquettes.

Vegetable croquettes

Ingredients: 400 g/¾ lb cooked soup vegetables, 4 eggs, 1 bunch parsley, 150 g/5 oz breadcrumbs, 150 g/5 oz flour, salt, pepper, cooking oil for frying

To prepare: Put the vegetables through a potato ricer or finely chop with a knife. Knead them together with 2 eggs, 2 tbsp breadcrumbs, salt, pepper, chopped parsley and sufficient flour to obtain a pliable dough. Shape finger-sized pieces from the dough, dip them into flour, beaten egg and breadcrumbs and fry them in hot cooking oil.

Smoked knuckle of pork with sauerkraut and beans

Ingredients

800–900 g/1¾–2 lb smoked knuckle of pork
600 g/1¼ lb sauerkraut
200 g/7 oz pinto beans
150 g/1 medium onion
1 bunch parsley, 15 g/1 tbsp lard
2 cloves garlic, salt

To prepare

Soak the beans for 1 day. Place the knuckle of pork into hot water, bring to the boil, drain and cook until tender in fresh water. Peel and thinly slice the onion.

To cook

Sauté the onion in the lard. Add the beans and sauté for a few minutes, then add the cooking liquor from the knuckle. When the beans are half done, add the sauerkraut and some more of the knuckle's cooking liquor if necessary. Season with crushed garlic and finely chopped parsley and cook until tender. Remove the meat from the bones, slice it and serve with bread-roll dumplings.

Bread-roll dumplings
Ingredients: 6 bread rolls, 2 eggs, 20 g/¾ oz breadcrumbs, 200 ml/1 cup milk, 1 bunch parsley, salt, ground black pepper
To prepare: Dice and scald the bread rolls with boiling milk. Knead together with the eggs, breadcrumbs, finely chopped parsley, salt and ground black pepper. Using your wet fingers, shape dumplings from this mixture and cook them for 15 minutes in salted water. Leave the dumplings in this water until ready to serve, or reheat them in it just prior to serving.

Calf's heart in game sauce

Ingredients

800 g/1¾ lb calf's or pig's hearts
50 g/3 slices smoked bacon
50 g/1 small onion
100 g/4 oz carrots
100 g/4 oz parsnips
200 ml/1 cup sour cream
1 tbsp mustard
200 ml/1 cup red wine, 1 lemon
1 tbsp flour
salt, peppercorn, thyme
bay leaf
coriander, marjoram
10 g/2 tsp granulated sugar

To prepare

Cut the hearts in half lengthwise, wash them to remove blood, then drain them. Trim the root vegetables and the onion and cut them into slices of equal thickness.

To cook

Dice and render the smoked bacon. Sear the hearts in this fat on both sides and set them aside. Using the same fat, caramelize a little sugar, and sauté the vegetables and the onion for a few minutes. Sprinkle with salt and add the red wine. Season with pepper, thyme, bay leaf, coriander and marjoram. Add 1 litre (2 pints) water and bring to the boil. Replace the seared hearts and cook them, under cover, until tender. Remove them once again and put the cooking liquor, together with the vegetables, through a blender or a fine sieve. Finally boil together with a smooth mixture of sour cream, mustard, lemon juice and a little flour. Pour this sauce over the sliced hearts and serve with bread-roll dumplings. For the bread-roll dumplings recipe see *Smoked knuckle of pork* (p 35.).

Chicken with cauliflower

Ingredients

900 g/2 lb chicken
500 g/1 lb cauliflower
300 g/¾ lb Savoy cabbage
80 g/3 oz onion
400 ml/1¾ cups sour cream,
1 tsp paprika paste
1 egg, salt, ground white pepper
50 g/2 oz butter

To prepare

Cut the chicken into 8 to 10 pieces. Sprinkle with salt and white pepper and sear both sides in hot butter.
Using the same butter, sauté the finely chopped onion, add 200 ml (1 cup) water and bring to the boil. Blanch the Savoy cabbage and separate the leaves. Boil the cauliflower in salted
water until half tender.

To cook

Line a skillet or oven-proof glass dish with Savoy cabbage leaves. Mound the half-cooked chicken and cauliflower florets on them. Pour a mixture of sour cream, paprika paste and raw egg on top. Roast in a moderate oven (170–190 °C/325–375 °F) until nicely browned.

Leg of rabbit with mushrooms

Ingredients

1 kg/2 lb rabbit legs
200 g/7 oz mushrooms
100 g/2 small onions
50 g/2 oz lard
30 g/2 tbsp butter
150 g/5 oz carrots
300 g/11 oz spaghetti
1 bunch parsley
3 tbsp flour, salt
ground white pepper
dash of saffron or turmeric

To prepare

Trim the mushrooms and cut them into wedges. Finely chop the onion and cut the carrots into thin strips.
Toss the carrots in butter for a few minutes. Add a little water, season with salt and pepper and simmer until tender. Before serving, mix and heat with cooked spaghetti and finely chopped parsley.

To cook

Salt the legs of rabbit, dip them into flour and sear both sides in hot fat. Set them aside. Using the same fat, sauté the onion, add the mushrooms and sauté until the juices released by the mushrooms have evaporated. Sprinkle with 1 tbsp flour and thin with ½ l (2¼ cups) cold water. Bring to the boil and replace the meat. Flavour with saffron and cook, over a low heat, until tender. Season with salt and pepper to taste. Serve with vegetable spaghetti.

Crispy roast pork

Ingredients

1–1.2 kg/2–3 lb leg of pork
(from a young animal)
150 g/about 8 slices smoked
bacon
3 cloves garlic, salt
200 ml/1 cup beer
600 g/1¼ lb red cabbage
150 g/2 medium onions
100 g/3½ oz lard
100 g/3½ oz granulated sugar
ground caraway seed
15 ml/1 tbsp vinegar
300 ml/1½ cups red wine
500 g/1 lb potatoes
ground black pepper
200 g/7 oz prunes
1 lemon, 1 stick cinnamon

To prepare

Trim and finely crush the garlic.
Combine with 1 tbsp salt and
rub the meat with this mixture
at least 1 hour before roasting.
Shred the cabbage, slice two-
thirds of the onion and finely
chop the rest of the onion. Boil
the potatoes in their skins, peel
and grate them.

To cook

Roast the meat in a very slow
oven (120–140 °C/250–275 °F)
for 55 to 60 minutes. Rub with
smoked bacon and baste with
beer during roasting. This is the
only way to achieve a reddish-
brown crackling on the crisp
roast with a "sheen". Use
a knife with a serrated blade to
carve the roast, removing the
meat from the bone. Serve with
sautéed cabbage, prunes cooked
in wine and fried grated
potatoes.
Sautéed cabbage: Sauté the
onion slices in 50 g (2 oz) lard.
Add the cabbage, season with
salt, sugar, caraway seed, vinegar and 200 ml (1 cup) of the
red wine and simmer until
tender.
Fried grated potatoes: Sauté the
rest of the onion in lard. Add
the grated potatoes, season with
salt and black pepper and
brown over a high heat.
Prunes cooked in wine: Cook
the prunes in 100 ml (½ cup)
red wine and water to cover for
15 minutes, having sweetened
them with sugar to taste, and
adding the juice of the lemon
and 1 stick cinnamon for
flavouring. Let the prunes cool
in their own juice.

Quince cake

Ingredients

700 g/1½ lb quince
350 g/12 oz granulated sugar
6 eggs, 250 g/8–9 oz flour
120 g/4 oz butter, 1 tsp rum
100 g/½ cup whipped cream
30 g/1 oz candied fruit, ½ lemon

To prepare

Grate the lemon rind and press out the juice. Pare the quince, cut them into wedges and remove the cores. Sweeten with 100 g (½ cup) granulated sugar and add the lemon juice. Add water to cover and cook for 15 minutes. Strain, chill and soak up excess moisture with a napkin.

To cook

Beat the eggs with 250 g (1 cup) sugar until creamy. Add the flour, grated lemon rind and finally the melted butter. Knead and leave to rest for ½ hour. Roll out the dough to a thickness of 2 cm (1 in) and line a baking pan or dish with it. Arrange quince wedges on top to make a star shape. Bake in a moderate oven (130–150 °C/ 230–300 °F) for ½ hour. Lift the cake out of the baking dish and leave to cool in a dry, cool place.
Serve sprinkled with rum and garnished with whipped cream. Arrange candied fruit—such as cranberries—over the whipped cream if you like.
This dessert will keep for 3 to 4 days in the refrigerator.

Ingredients

400 g/14 oz pickled fish
200 g/2 medium tomatoes
200 g/7 oz cucumber
1 lemon, 80 g/3 oz butter
50 g/2 oz olives, 1 bunch chives
500 g/1 lb French bread or croissants
salt, ground black pepper

To prepare

Fillet the fish. Cut the fillets into slices about 2 cm (1 in) thick or into flat slices. Thinly slice the tomatoes and cucumber and season them with salt and pepper.

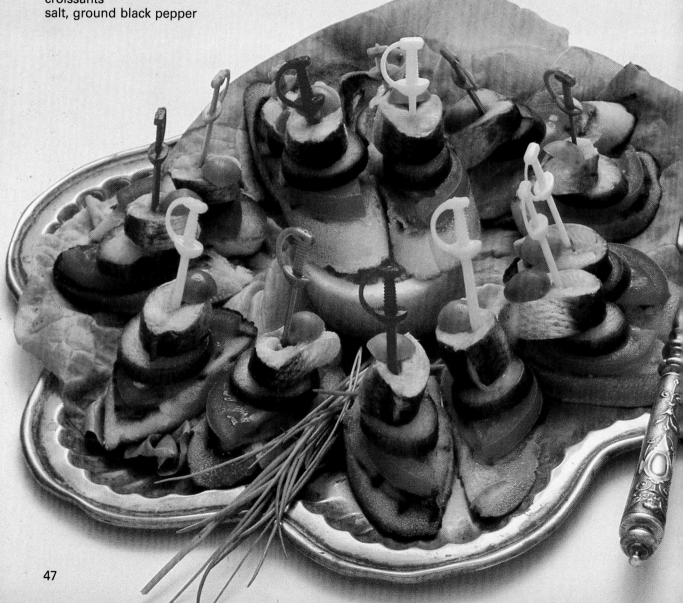

To cook

Toast the thinly sliced bread or croissants and spread them with butter. Place on each slice a slice of tomato, cucumber and fish and top with an olive. Finally, sprinkle with lemon juice, then with finely chopped chives, stick a toothpick or plastic pick in them and serve immediately.

Pickled fish bites

Chicken goulash

Ingredients

1(800–900 g/1 ½–2 lbs) chicken
100 g/2 small onions
100 g/4 oz carrots
100 g/4 oz parsnips
50 g/2 oz celeriac
200 g/7 oz potatoes
100 g/4 oz green peppers
100 g/1 medium tomato
50 g/2 oz lard
3 cloves garlic, 2 tsp hot paprika
1 hot green pepper (or chili powder), salt
1 egg, 50 g/2 oz flour

To prepare

Cut the trimmed chicken into 40/50 g (1 ½–2 oz) pieces. Finely chop the onion, dice the root vegetables, the potatoes, the green peppers and the tomato. Thinly slice the hot green pepper. Combine the egg with a dash of salt and the flour, to make a stiff dough. Tear off tiny dumplings (*csipetke*), cover with a napkin and set aside.

To cook

Sauté the onion in a little fat, sprinkle with paprika and immediately pour in 100 ml (½ cup) water. Add the green peppers, vegetables, the tomato and add water to cover. Bring to the boil, then season with salt, hot paprika and crushed garlic. Add the pieces of chicken and the potatoes. By the time the chicken is cooked there should be about 5 cm (2 in) of cooking liquid over the meat. Just before serving, add the *csipetke* dumplings and cook for a few more minutes. Serve immediately. (This dish is a soup, not a stew.)

Lentil salad

Ingredients

300 g/¾ lb lentils
250 g/½ lb carrots
200 g/scant ½ lb leeks
1 bunch parsley, salt, pepper
cooking oil, wine vinegar, sugar

To prepare

Wash the lentils and soak for
1 to 2 hours, then cook them in
salted water. Pare the carrots
and the leeks and cut them into
thin rings. Finely chop the parsley. Salt the carrots and leeks,
leave to stand for ½ hour, then
drain off the juices released.
Prepare salad dressing from
½ l (1 pt) cup water: season
with salt, pepper, sugar and
vinegar, sprinkle with parsley
and cooking oil. Combine the
cooked and drained lentils, the
carrots and the onion. Pour the
dressing over them and chill in
the refrigerator for 1 to 2 hours.
This salad keeps for a long time.
Serve as an accompaniment to
roast poultry and lamb.

Saddle of rabbit with garlic

Ingredients

1 (900 g/2 lb) saddle of rabbit
2 bread rolls
100 g/4 oz grated cheese
2 bunch parsley
5 cloves garlic, salt, pepper
400 g/¾ lb spinach
200 g/6 baby onions
100 g/4 oz carrots
100 g/4 oz parsnips
100 g/4 oz butter, 50 g/2 oz lard

To prepare

Remove the thin skin from the rabbit. Make incisions on both sides lengthwise along the backbone. Salt and lightly brush with melted butter. Roast in a moderate oven (170–190 °C/ 350–375 °F) for 35 to 40 minutes. Trim, wash, scald and drain the spinach. Directly before serving flavour with crushed garlic and sauté in 30 g (2 tbsp) butter. Trim and julienne the carrots and the parsnips and cook them in salted water. Drain and toss in 30 g (2 tbsp) butter before serving. Peel the onions, gash the tops, taking care that they remain in one piece. Season and roast alongside the meat in the oven.

To cook

Grate the bread rolls (do not use packaged breadcrumbs!). Combine with the grated cheese, finely chopped garlic, parsley, a dash of salt, pepper and 2 tbsp butter. Roast this mixture in 2 to 3 layers over the tender saddle of rabbit. Roast for another 5 minutes after the final layer has been added.
Carve the meat carefully and serve with the leaf spinach, roast onions and buttered vegetables.

Sausage baked in pastry

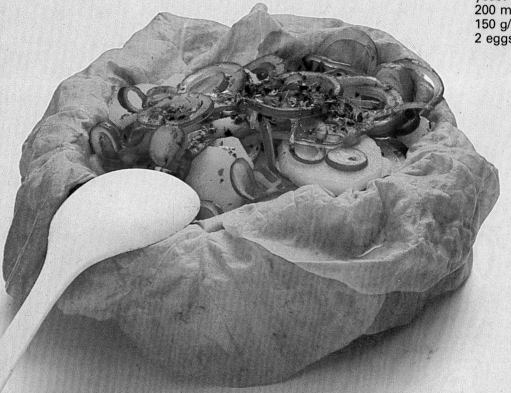

Ingredients

400 g/¾ lb lightly smoked
sausage
450 g/1 lb flour, 25 g/2 packages
yeast (compressed)
200 ml/1 cup milk
150 g/5 oz butter
2 eggs, salt, sugar

To prepare

Crumble the yeast into
lukewarm milk, sprinkle in
a dash of sugar, mix into the
flour, cover with a cloth napkin
and allow to rise in a warm
place for 30 to 40 minutes.

To cook

Roll out the dough on a floured
board to a thickness of 1 cm
(½ in) and cut it up into strips
3 cm (1 in) wide.
Roll each strip around a chunk
of sausage. Place these into
a baking pan and spread the
tops with beaten egg. Bake in
moderate oven for 15 to 20
minutes. Serve with a seasonal
salad. This dish is also excellent
when served cold.

Roast duck with cabbage and chestnuts

Ingredients

1 (1–1.2 kg/2–3 lb) duck
80 g (1 medium) onion
150 g/5 oz onion, shredded
50 g/2 oz lard, 200 g/7 oz shelled
baked chestnuts
300 g/¾ lb apples
400 g/¾–1 lb red cabbage
100 ml/½ cup red wine
1 bunch parsley, salt, marjoram
ground caraway seed
15 ml/1 tbsp vinegar
15 g/1 tbsp granulated sugar

To prepare

Trim and draw the duck and rub it with salt both inside and out. Sprinkle marjoram into the abdominal cavity and place in it an onion cut in half and parsley. Place in a pre-heated oven and roast without the addition of lard and water. Baste the duck frequently with its own fat. When the meat is half done, cover with aluminium foil and continue roasting until the meat is tender and the skin brown and crisp.
Shred the red cabbage and the remaining onion. Cut the apple in half but do not skin it. Remove the core, then cut the apple into wedges. Coarsely chop the shelled baked chestnuts.

To cook

Melt the granulated sugar in a little fat. Sauté the onion in it, sprinkle with ground caraway seed. Add the cabbage, season lightly with salt and, stirring frequently, simmer until the cabbage becomes limp. Now add the red wine, the apples and the chestnuts. Cook until tender and serve, seasoned with salt, vinegar and sugar, as a garnish to the crispy roast duck.

Chicken and vegetable casserole

Ingredients

1 (800–900 g/1¾–2 lb) chicken
100 g/1 medium onion
200 g/7 oz carrots
400 g/14 oz Brussels sprouts
200 g/7 oz mushrooms
2 cloves garlic, salt, ground
black pepper
50 g/2 oz lard, thyme
1 bunch parsley

To prepare

Cut the chicken into 10–12
pieces. Trim the vegetables. Cut
the onion and the mushrooms
into wedges and the carrots into
thin rings. Finely chop the parsley and trim and wash the Brussels sprouts.

To cook

Combine the prepared ingredients, sprinkle with a little melted
butter and season with salt,
black pepper and thyme. Soak
an earthenware casserole in
water, then place the prepared
ingredients in it and roast in a
hot oven for 1 to 1½ hours.

Roast lamb in red wine

Ingredients

800 g/1¾ lb leg or shoulder of lamb, boned
100 g/4 oz carrots
100 g/4 oz parsnips
50 g/2 oz celeriac
100 g/2 small onions
50 g/2 oz lard
salt, peppercorn, bay leaf, thyme
30 g/2 tbsp tomato paste
300 ml/1½ cups red wine
200 ml/1 cup cream
75 g/1 tbsp flour

To prepare

Trim and slice the root vegetables and the onion.

To cook

Salt the meat. Sear both sides in hot lard and set aside. Using the same fat, sauté the sliced vegetables and the onion. Add the tomato paste, blend thoroughly, continue sautéing for a few more minutes, then thin with red wine. Season with bay leaf, thyme, salt and pepper and bring to the boil. Now replace the seared meat and simmer, covered, over a low heat until tender. Add 100 ml (½ cup) water occasionally if necessary. When the meat is done, remove from the pan gravy and carve. Strain the gravy and rub the vegetables through a sieve. Heat them up once again and boil together with a smooth paste of cream and flour. Season to taste and pour the sauce over the meat. Serve with potato croquettes.

Potato croquettes

Ingredients: 300 g/10 oz potatoes, 4 eggs, 150 g/5 oz flour, 80 g/3 oz breadcrumbs, salt, ground nutmeg, 300 ml/1¼ cups cooking oil for frying
To prepare: Peel and dice the potatoes. Boil in salted water, drain, then rub through a sieve. Work together with 100 g (1 cup) flour, 2 eggs, salt and nutmeg. Shape finger-sized sticks from the dough, dip each into flour, egg and breadcrumbs and fry in hot cooking oil until brown.

1. Sear the meat in a little lard...
2. Using the same fat sauté the vegetables...
3. Stir in the tomato paste...
4. Add a little water and the red wine, and start to cook.

Smoked breast of goose with apple purée

Ingredients

600–700 g/1¼–1½ lb smoked breast of goose, boned
400 g/¾ lb apples, Jonathan variety
500 g/1 lb pears, Alexander variety
500 g/1 lb potatoes, 1 lemon
50 g/2 oz butter
200 ml/1 cup dry white wine
1 tbsp sugar
salt, cloves, cinnamon
200 ml/1 cup milk

To prepare

Soak the breast of goose for 24 hours, drain off the liquid, put in fresh cold water and cook over a low flame until tender. Keep in the liquid until serving time.

To cook

Cut the pears into wedges (but do not pare them). Cut out the core and lightly sauté the pears in the rest of the butter and a little white wine for 4 to 5 minutes. Serve immediately with the thinly sliced hot breast of goose, hot mashed potatoes and cold apple purée.

Apple purée

Pare the apples and remove the cores. Boil them in 100 ml (½ cup) wine, a little sweetened and flavoured water, with sugar, lemon juice, cloves, cinnamon, for 10–15 minutes. Rub through a fine sieve and chill.

Mashed potatoes

Skin and dice the potatoes. Boil them in salted water, drain and mash. Beat with 2 tbsp butter and a dash of salt, then slowly stir in the hot milk.

Cheese pudding

Ingredients

200 g/7 oz grated Parmesan cheese
3 bread rolls, 2 eggs
120 g/4 oz butter, salt, nutmeg

To prepare

Remove crust from the bread rolls, dry in a warm place, then grate.

To cook

Beat 100 g (3½ oz) soft butter until creamy. Beat in the 2 whole eggs one after the other, combine with the grated cheese and then with the breadcrumbs. Season with salt and nutmeg. Pour this mixture into a buttered dish and place over steam in a low oven (110–130 °C/ 230–270 °F) for 40 to 45 minutes. Turn out of the dish, slice and serve immediately with almond sauce.

Almond sauce

Ingredients: 150 g/5 oz blanched almonds, 200 ml/1 cup cream, 3 egg yolks, salt, ground white pepper
To cook: Pound the almonds in a mortar. Add the cream and egg yolks and, stirring constantly, thicken this mixture in a double saucepan. Remove from the heat and continue stirring. Season with salt and white pepper and serve hot.

Jellied pork

Ingredients (Serves 8)

1 (900 g/2 lb) smoked knuckle
of pork
1 (800 g/1¾ lb) raw knuckle
of pork
150 g/3 small onions
100 g/4 oz carrots
150 g/5 oz parsnips
100 g/4 oz celeriac
1 head garlic, peppercorn

To prepare

Soak the smoked knuckle of
pork in cold water for 24 hours.
Plunge into boiling water for
5 to 6 minutes, then cool in cold
water. Trim the vegetables, garlic and onion and cut them into
long wedges.

To cook

Place the two knuckles in 3 litres
(3 quarts) cold water, slowly
bring to the boil, then skim carefully. Add the vegetables, onion,
garlic and peppercorns and cook
over a low heat until the raw
knuckle is completely done.
Remove the meat from the bone
and arrange on eight serving
plates.
When the smoked knuckle is
tender, lift it out of cooking
liquor, remove the meat from
the bone and arrange it on
plates. Strain the crystal clear
golden stock through a fine
sieve. Blot fat from the top,
using a paper napkin to soak off
even the tiniest grease spot.
Place some of the cooked carrots alongside the meat if you
like. Pour the cooking liquor into
plates and chill until the stock is
firm. Keep in the refrigerator
until serving time.
Sprinkled with lemon juice or
wine vinegar, jellied pork is an
irresistible dish.
NB. The water which evaporates
during cooking must be
constantly replaced.

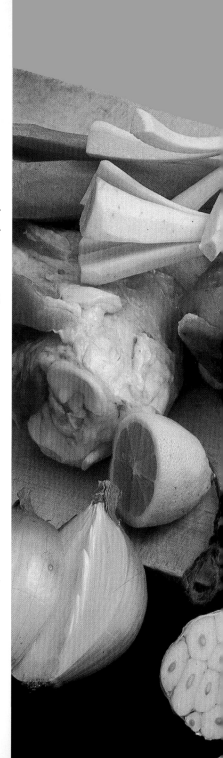

Lentil soup with sausage

Ingredients

150 g/5 oz lentils
200 g/7 oz smoked sausage
50 g/1 small onion
100 g/4 oz carrots, diced
100 g/4 oz parsnips, diced
50 g/2 oz celeriac, diced
3 cloves garlic
1 tbsp mustard, salt, ground
black pepper
2 tbsp wine vinegar
2 bay leaves
7 g/1 tbsp flour, 15 g/1 tbsp lard
200 ml/1 cup sour cream

To prepare

Wash and soak the lentils in water for ½ hour. Trim and dice the carrots, celeriac and parsnips, finely chop the onion and thinly slice the sausage. (Soak the sausage in lukewarm water for a few minutes for easy skinning.)

To cook

Start cooking the lentils in 1 litre (1 quart) cold water and simmer until half done. Add the prepared vegetables, bay leaves and sausage. Season with a dash of salt. Lightly brown the flour in the lard, toss in the finely chopped onions and remove from heat. Stir in the crushed garlic, mustard and sour cream. Pour this mixture into the soup and boil for a few minutes. Before serving, season to taste with salt, ground black pepper and wine vinegar.

Cabbage salad with ketchup

Ingredients

600 g/1¼ lb cabbage
250 g/½ lb leeks
200 ml/1 cup ketchup
100 ml/½ cup olive oil
salt, ground caraway seed
1 head lettuce

To prepare

Cut the cabbage in half, remove core and shred. Mix with 1 tsp salt, leave to stand for 20 minutes, then squeeze out excess moisture. Slice the leeks.

To cook

Combine the ketchup with the olive oil and the ground caraway seed, then add the cabbage and the leeks. Arrange in a bowl lined with lettuce leaves. Serve thoroughly chilled, but remember that this salad is at its best while the cabbage is still firm.
Serve with roasts.

Hare in game sauce

Ingredients

1 kg/2 lb 2 legs and
2 shoulders of hare
80 g/4 or 5 slices smoked bacon,
100 g/4 oz carrots
100 g/4 oz parsnips
50 g/2 oz celeriac
1 lemon, 50 g/1 small onion
200 ml/1 cup sour cream
1 tbsp mustard
300 g/¾ lb (about 2) oranges
salt, peppercorn, bay leaf
thyme
200 ml/1 cup dry white wine

To prepare

Lard the leg of hare with thin
strips of bacon. Trim and thinly
slice the vegetables and the
onion.
Peel the oranges and cut into
wedges, removing the pith.

To cook

Render the rest of the bacon
and sear the meat in its fat.
Season with salt and set aside.
In the remaining fat sauté the
onion and root vegetables.
Season with pepper, bay leaf
and thyme and bring to the boil
with 200 ml (1 cup) white wine
and 300 ml (1¼ cups) water.
Add the meat and cook, covered, over a low heat, until tender. Remove the meat once
again and put the cooking liquor, together with the vegetables through a sieve or blender. Combine with the smooth
mixture of flour, mustard, lemon
juice and sour cream. Bring to
the boil once again and pour
over the meat. Serve decorated
with wedges of orange and garnished with potato noodles.

Potato noodles

Ingredients: 500 g/1 lb potatoes
250 g/8 oz flour, 1 egg
100 g/2 small onions
50 g/2 oz lard, salt
To prepare: Boil the potatoes in
their skins, peel and mash them
while still hot and work together
with the flour, egg and a dash of
salt. Cut into pieces 2–3 cm
(1 in) wide and 3–4 cm (2 in)
long. Shape into cylindrical
pieces and boil in salted water
for a few minutes. Drain it
thoroughly. Toss in the hot fat in
which the finely chopped onion
has been sautéed.

Minced breast of goose

Ingredients

1 kg/2 lb breast of goose
300 g/11 oz green peppers
600 g/1¼ lb potatoes
200 g/7 oz leeks
2 cloves garlic
salt
ground black pepper, marjoram
1 egg

To prepare

Peel the potatoes and cut them into wedges. Slice the green peppers and the leeks. Remove the meat from the breast of goose, grind together with its fatty skin. Season with salt, black pepper, crushed garlic and marjoram. Work together with 1 egg, and shaping the mixture with wet fingers, replace over breast bone.

To cook

Season the potatoes, leeks and green peppers with salt and pepper and place in a soaked earthenware casserole. Arrange the breast of goose on top, cover and roast in a hot oven for about 1 hour.
Remove the meat from the bone, slice and serve garnished with roast potatoes.

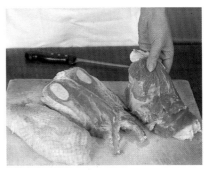

1–2. Bone the meat...
3. Replace the minced and seasoned meat over the breast-bone with wet fingers
4. Flatten with a knife dipped in water or wet fingers.

Quails with juniper

Ingredients

8 quails, 100 g/6 slices smoked bacon
500 g/1 lb Savoy cabbage
200 g/7 oz carrots
200 g/7 oz parsnips, salt
ground juniper berries
30 g/2 tbsp lard
50 g/2 oz butter, allspice

To prepare

Trim and draw the quails, salt both inside and outside and sprinkle with ground juniper. Remove the core from the Savoy, and boil the cabbage in salted water for 2 to 3 minutes. Cut off the thicker ribs from the outer leaves.
Trim and julienne the carrots and parsnips. Boil them in salted water, then drain. Toss in hot butter just before serving and season to taste with salt and allspice.

To cook

Wrap each quail separately in thin strips of bacon and Savoy cabbage leaves. Arrange them in a lightly greased roasting pan, cover with foil and roast in a pre-heated oven (200 °C/ 400 °F) for 40 to 45 minutes. Serve piping hot with the vegetables.

Lamb bites

Ingredients

600 g/1¼ lb lamb, boned
50 g/1 small onion
1 bunch parsley
4 cloves garlic
300 g/11 oz green peppers
100 ml/½ cup cooking oil
50 g/2 oz butter
salt, ground black pepper
ground rosemary, hot paprika
1 bunch chives
800 g/1¾ lb potatoes
100 ml/½ cup dry white wine
½ tbsp flour

To prepare

Wash the potatoes, salt them and wrap individually in aluminium foil. Bake them in a hot oven. Dice the green peppers and finely chop the onion, chives and parsley.

To cook

Grind the meat, then knead with salt, pepper, crushed garlic, rosemary, hot paprika and the parsley. Shape small sausage-shaped pieces with wet fingers, place them in a roasting pan coated with cooking oil and bake in a hot oven (200 °C/400 °F) for 25 to 30 minutes. Serve with roast/baked potatoes and paprika sauce.

Paprika sauce

Sauté the onion and the green peppers in butter. Season with salt and pepper and sprinkle with flour. Thin with 100 ml (½ cup) white wine and a little water and reduce to sauce consistency. Sprinkle with chopped chives before serving.

Larded fillet of beef with mushroom sauce

Ingredients

600 g/1¼ lb fillet of beef
100 g/6 slices smoked bacon
200 ml/1 cup cooking oil for the
marinade
salt, ground black pepper
1 bunch parsley
400 g/14 oz Brussels sprouts
40 g/3 tbsp butter
fat for frying

To prepare

Remove the thin skin from the
meat and marinate in cooking
oil for 2 to 3 days (place in
a plastic bag, pour the cooking
oil over it, seal the bag securely
and place in the refrigerator).
Drain off the oil from the meat
before cooking, lard with thin
strips of smoked bacon, season
with salt and pepper and sear
both sides in hot fat for 3–4
minutes. Toss the trimmed Brussels sprouts in a little butter,
season with salt and cook,
covered, until tender in 200–300
ml (1 to 1½ cups) water.

1. Combine the mashed potatoes first with the
egg and afterwards with the flour...
2. Rub your palm with cooking oil and shape
the dough with the help of a spoon...
3. Fry in hot cooking oil until brown.

To cook

Place the meat in hot oven
(250–280 °C/450–550 °F) and
roast according to taste: 10
minutes for rare, 15 minutes for
medium and 30 minutes for well
done. Slice with a sharp knife
and serve garnished with
sautéed Brussels sprouts, potato
cakes and mushroom sauce
made with red wine.

Mushroom sauce

Ingredients: 200 g/7 oz
mushrooms, 50 g/1 small onion,
50 g/3 tbsp tomato paste,
1 tsp flour, 200 ml/1 cup red
wine, cooking oil, salt, ground
black pepper, 1 bunch parsley,
1 bunch chives
To prepare: Sauté the finely
chopped onion and the trimmed, sliced mushrooms in a little hot cooking oil. When all the
juices released by the mushrooms have evaporated sprinkle with flour, stir in the tomato
paste and thin with the red
wine. Season with salt and
ground black pepper and add
the finely chopped parsley and
chives. Reduce to sauce consistency.

Potato cakes

Ingredients: 500 g/1 lb potatoes,
2 eggs, 80 g/3 oz flour, salt, nutmeg, oil for frying.
To prepare: Boil, peel and mash
the potatoes. Season with salt
and grated nutmeg, then work
together with egg and flour.
Using a tablespoon, cut away
chunks from this dough and fry
in hot cooking oil.

Martinmas fare

Ingredients

300 g/10 oz fresh liver sausage
300 g/10 oz blood sausage
300 g/10 oz garlic sausages
500 g/1 lb potatoes
500 g/1 lb red cabbage
100 g/2 small onions
salt, marjoram, caraway seed
granulated sugar
2 tbsp vinegar, 50 g/2 oz butter
50 g/2 oz lard
100 ml/½ cup red wine

To prepare

Thinly slice the cabbage and onions. Peel the potatoes, cut them into small cubes, boil them in salted water, then drain. Season with marjoram and toss in hot butter before serving.

Sautéed cabbage

Melt 2 tsp sugar in 1 tbsp lard. Sauté the onions in this, sprinkle with caraway seed, then add the cabbage and season with salt. Sauté the cabbage until limp, then sprinkle with red wine and vinegar and simmer until tender.

Liver sausage, blood sausage and garlic sausages

Place these into a hot roasting pan greased with lard. Put into a hot oven and roast for 20 to 25 minutes. Baste frequently with the fatty pan juices. (Avoid exposure to moisture or the skins will burst.) Cut the sausages into 30/40 g (½ oz) pieces. Serve with potatoes flavoured with marjoram and sautéed cabbage.

Chestnut pudding

Ingredients

300 g/10 oz shelled chestnuts
or chestnut purée
2 eggs, 4 bread rolls
100 g/3½–4 oz butter
50 g/2 oz granulated sugar
grated nutmeg

To prepare

Put the chestnuts through
a potato ricer.
Remove the crust from the
bread rolls and cut the centres
into very small cubes.

1. Combine the creamy butter with egg...
2. Knead together with chestnuts and the
diced bread rolls...
3. And fill a metal mold with this mixture.

To cook

Beat soft butter until creamy.
One by one add the eggs, then
lightly fold in the riced chestnuts. Now fold in the bread
cubes. Season with nutmeg and
sugar and arrange in a lightly
buttered dish.
Place the dish in a baking pan
half-filled with water and bake in
moderate oven (170–190 °C/
325–375 °F) for 35 to 40 minutes.
Turn out of the mold, slice and
serve with chocolate sauce or
whipped cream.

Chocolate sauce

Ingredients: 200 g/7 oz dark
chocolate, 200 ml/1 cup cream,
dash rum.
Stirring constantly bring the
chocolate to the boil in the
cream. Remove from heat, then
stir in the rum and serve
immediately.

Cheese salad

Ingredients

300 g/about ¾ lb (6 slices)
Gruyère or other hard cheese
150 g/5 oz leeks
200 g/7 oz green peppers
150 g/2 small tomatoes
150 g/5 oz cucumber
200 ml/1 cup sour cream
1 tbsp paprika paste
salt, ground black pepper

To prepare

Trim and wash the leeks,
cucumber and the green peppers and slice them thin. Cut the
tomatoes into wedges and the
cheese into thin slices. Salt the
onion, cucumber and green peppers, leave them to stand for 10
minutes, then drain off the
juices released.

To cook

Blend the sour cream with the
paprika paste until smooth.
Carefully stir in the leeks,
cheese, green peppers,
cucumber and the tomatoes.
Season according to taste with
salt and pepper and serve cold
as an entrée.
Also an excellent vitamin-rich
supper dish for weight-
watchers.

Cream of hare soup

Ingredients

350–400 g/¾ lb hare trimmings
(whatever is left of the carcase
after removing the saddle and
the legs)
50 g/1 small onion, 100 g/4 oz
carrots, 100 g/4 oz parsnips
50 g/2 oz celeriac, 2 bay leaves
salt, peppercorn
150 g/5 oz mushrooms
30 g/2 tbsp butter, 200 ml/1 cup
cream, 1 egg, 3 g/1 tbsp breadcrumbs

To prepare

Bring the hare trimmings to the
boil in 1 litre (1 quart) cold
water. Skim, then add the trimmed and sliced mushrooms, the
cleansed and cut up vegetables
and the onion. Season with salt,
peppercorn and bay leaves and
simmer over a low heat until the
meat is done.

To cook

Strain the soup. Slice the
cooked soup vegetables and set
aside. Remove meat from the
bones, grind or very finely chop
with a sharp knife. Combine the
ground meat with the egg,
breadcrumbs and soft butter.
Season with salt and pepper
and, using a teaspoon, drop
dumpling-sized pieces into the
boiling soup. Simmer for 5 minutes. Add the cream, the sliced
soup vegetables and the mushrooms and bring to the boil
once again before serving.

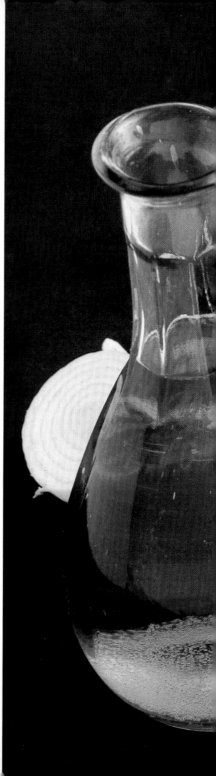

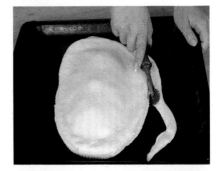

Feast sealed in pastry

Ingredients

Stuffing
200 g/7 oz chicken liver
8 quail's eggs
300 g/10 oz leg of veal
250 g/8 oz mushrooms
1 bunch parsley
50 g/1 small onion, salt, ground
black pepper
50 g/2 oz butter, marjoram

Pastry
600 g/1¼ lb flour
300 g/10 oz butter
dash salt, 1 egg, beaten
175 ml/¾ cup water
1 egg, for brushing

To prepare

Work the flour, salt and butter together, add the egg and cold water and knead to obtain a smooth dough. Leave to rest in the refrigerator for ½ hour. Remove the thin skin from the veal and cut into very small cubes. Sauté the finely chopped onion in butter, turn the meat in this, and add the mushrooms cut into wedges. Season with salt and pepper and simmer until tender. Remove from the heat, leave to cool, then combine with the diced raw chicken liver and the boiled quail's eggs. Season with marjoram, salt and chopped parsley. Drain the stuffing to reduce the quantity of lard and water to the minimum.

To cook

Divide the dough into two equal parts and roll out to a thickness of 1–2 cm (½ in). Place in a lightly buttered roasting pan, brush with egg and heap the stuffing over the middle. Cover with the other half of the dough and press the edges together. Use the pastry trimmings to make decorations. Using a sharp knife, cut a hole with a diameter of 2 cm (1 in) on top. Brush with egg and bake in a moderate oven (170–190 °C/ 350–375 °F) for 45 to 50 minutes. Serve immediately with a seasonal salad.

1. Roll out the pastry divided into two equal parts to a thickness of 2–3 cm (2 in)...
2–3. Heap the filling over the middle, brush the edges with egg, use the other sheet of dough to cover...
4. Shape and decorate the edges with your finger.

Ingredients

800–900 g/1¾–2 lb smoked
knuckle of pork
400 g/¾ lb spinach
300 g/11 oz canned corn
200 ml/1 cup cream
2 tbsp dry mustard
4 tbsp grated pickled
horseradish
2 cloves garlic, 40 g/3 tbsp butter
salt, ground white pepper
100 ml/½ cup cooking oil
½ lemon, 100 ml/½ cup white
wine, 1 bunch parsley

To prepare

Soak the knuckle in lukewarm
water for 1 to 2 hours before
cooking. Start cooking the meat
in fresh cold water, over a very
low heat, at just below simmer-
ing point. Remove the meat
from the bone before serving
and carve it. Trim, wash, scald
and drain the spinach.

To cook

Blend the mustard with a dash
of salt, pepper and the lemon
juice until smooth. Stirring constantly, trickle in the oil very
slowly. Thin with white wine
and stir in the pickled horseradish.
Drain the canned corn, toss in
hot butter, sprinkle with finely
chopped parsley and add the
cream. Cook until the cream is
reduced to half its original
volume. Season with salt and
pepper and serve hot.
Toss the scalded spinach in
2 tbsp hot butter. Season with
salt, crushed garlic and black
pepper and serve as a garnish
with the cooked knuckle of pork,
the creamy corn and the cold
horseradish-mustard sauce.

92

Smoked knuckle of pork, gourmet style

Roast pork with vegetable molds

Ingredients

800 g/1¾ lb spareribs or
shoulder of pork
30 g/2 tbsp lard
65 g/5 tbsp butter
150 g/5 oz green peas
150 g/5 oz carrots
150 g/5 oz red cabbage
shredded, 50 ml/¼ cup cream
3 eggs, salt, ground white
pepper, ground nutmeg
ground caraway seed
4 cloves garlic

To prepare

Lard the meat generously with
thin wedges of garlic, season
with salt, rub with lard and
sprinkle with ground caraway
seed. Roast in a moderate oven
(170–190 °C/325–375 °F) for 45
to 50 minutes. Baste frequently
with lard. After a crust has
formed on the surface of the
meat, cover it with aluminium
foil and continue roasting. When
the meat is tender, carve it and
serve it with a variety of
vegetable molds.

Vegetable molds
Thinly slice the carrots and
lightly sauté them in 1 tbsp butter. Add a little water and simmer. Rub them through a fine
sieve or chop with a knife to
pulp consistency. Season with
salt, ground white pepper and
nutmeg. Stirring constantly,
trickle in 1 tbsp cream. Finally,
beat in 1 raw egg. Fill lightly
buttered metal bowls or coffee
cups with this mixture. Stand
these in a roasting pan half-filled
with water, put into the oven
and steam for 20 to 25 minutes.
Turn out and serve piping hot.
Follow the same recipe to make
molds from green peas, red cabbage, or any other kind of vegetable using 150 g (5 oz) trimmed vegetable of your choice,
1 egg, 1 tbsp cream and 2 tbsp
butter.

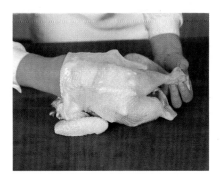

Stuffed chicken, Újházi style

Ingredients

1 (800–900 g/1¾–2 lb) chicken
40 g/1 small onion
1 bunch parsley
50 g/2 oz mushrooms
60 g/4 tbsp lard
50 g/2 oz home-made vermicelli
salt, ground black pepper
50 g/3 tbsp paprika paste
300 g/11 oz rice, 1 egg

To prepare

Trim and finely chop the onion, the parsley and the mushrooms. Cook the vermicelli in salted water, drain, spray with cold water to cool, then drain again.

To cook

Sauté the onion in 1 tbsp lard, then add the mushrooms and sauté them until the released juices have evaporated. Sprinkle with parsley, season with salt and pepper. Remove from the heat, leave to cool for a little while, then combine with 1 raw egg and finally with the vermicelli. Salt the abdominal cavity and the back of the chicken, stuff the filling under the loose skin and roast in a moderate oven (170–190°C/350–375°F) for 45 to 50 minutes. Baste the bird frequently with the pan juices. Remove from oven, leave to stand for 8 to 10 minutes, then carve and serve with rice Hungarian style and stewed fruits.

Rice, Hungarian style

Heat the rice in 1 tbsp lard. Add ½ litre (2¼ cups) boiling water and stir in the paprika paste. Bring to the boil, cover and remove from heat. Leave to stand for 20 minutes without stirring.

1. Loosen the skin of the chicken starting from the neck...
2–3. Arrange the stuffing uniformly under the skin...
4. Secure with a skewer to prevent the stuffing from being pressed out during cooking.

Beef stew with tomatoes

Ingredients

800 g/1¾ lb shin of beef
200 g/7 oz mushrooms
250 g/8–9 oz celeriac
4 cloves garlic
100 g/6 tbsp tomato paste, *or*
200 g/2 small fresh tomatoes
50 g/2 oz lard, 100 g/4 oz onion, finely chopped
200 ml/1 cup red wine
600 g/1¼ lb potatoes
1 bunch parsley
40 g/3 tbsp butter

To prepare

Wash and dice the meat. Trim the celeriac and cut it into tiny cubes. Wash the mushrooms and cut them into wedges. Finely chop the onion. Dip the tomatoes into boiling water for 15 to 20 seconds, then skin them. Leave them to cool, then finely chop them.

To cook

Lightly sauté the onion in lard. Place the meat on top of it and, stirring constantly, sauté it over high heat. Pour in the red wine and add the tomatoes. Season with salt and crushed garlic. Add a little water from time to time. When the meat is half done, add the celeriac and the mushrooms. Cook until the meat is tender and serve with parsley-buttered potatoes.

Parsley potatoes

Skin and dice the potatoes, cook them in salted water, then drain them. Sauté parsley in hot butter, toss the potatoes in it and serve immediately.

Saddle of hare with bread-roll pudding

Ingredients

1 (900–950 g/2–3 lb) saddle
of hare
50 g/3 slices smoked bacon
50 g/1 small onion
100 g/4 oz carrots
100 g/4 oz parsnips
50 g/2 oz celeriac
50 g/3 tbsp tomato paste
200 ml/1 cup red wine
200 ml/1 cup cooking oil
1 tbsp granulated sugar
salt, peppercorn, bay leaf
thyme

To prepare

Remove the thin skin from the
meat, place the hare in a plastic
bag, sprinkle with cooking oil,
seal securely and marinate in
the refrigerator for 2 days. Drain
off the oil from the meat, and
lard with strips of smoked
bacon. Season with salt and
place in a hot oven for 5
minutes until a uniform grey
crust forms on the meat.
Trim and thinly slice the
vegetables and the onion.

To cook

Brown the sugar in 50 ml
(¼ cup) cooking oil, add the
root vegetables and onion. Season with salt and brown for
a few more minutes. Add the tomato paste and thin with red
wine. Bring to the boil, then add
the seared saddle of hare and
cook, covered, until tender. Remove the meat and put the
cooking liquor, together with the
vegetables, through a blender.
Thin with a little water if necessary. Bone and slice the meat
and serve topped with the hot
sauce. Garnish with bread-roll
pudding.

Bread-roll pudding

Ingredients: 6 bread rolls,
2 eggs, 1 bunch parsley, 2 tbsp
breadcrumbs, 200 ml/1 cup milk,
50 g/2 oz lard, salt, ground black
pepper
Dice the bread rolls and scald
with milk. Season with salt,
pepper and chopped parsley
and knead with the eggs and
the breadcrumbs. Wrap in
a lightly buttered cloth napkin,
tie up and cook in salted water
for 20 minutes. Cut into slices
2–3 cm (1 in) thick and serve
immediately.

1. Cut the raised and rolled-out pastry into strips using a rolling pin and wrap around a cream-horn tin dipped in cooking oil...
2. Fry in hot cooking oil or lard...
3. Fill with chestnuts when cool.

Ingredients

500 g/18 oz flour
80 g/3 oz butter
300 ml/1½ cups milk
1 tsp granulated sugar
30 g/2 packages yeast (compressed), 3 egg yolks
salt, 250 g/8–9 oz chestnut purée, 200 ml/1 cup cream
150 g/5 oz canned sour cherries
1 l/1 quart cooking oil for frying
50 g/2 oz confectioner's sugar

To prepare

Crumble the yeast into 100 ml (½ cup) lukewarm milk and mix with a dash of granulated sugar and 1 tsp flour. Cover with a cloth napkin and leave to rise in a warm place for 20 to 25 minutes. Now work in the egg yolk, the flour, the melted butter, the rest of the milk and a dash of salt. Work the dough well. When blisters 2–3 cm (1 in) in diameter start to appear on the surface, cover with a cloth napkin and leave to rise in a warm place for 40 minutes. Roll out on floured board to a thickness of 1–2 cm (½ in) and cut into strips 3 cm (1 in) wide. Wind the strips of dough around a metallic cone-shaped (cream horn) mold and fry them individually in hot cooking oil. Instead of frying the strips of dough in oil you may wind them round the molds or cone-shaped pieces of wood and bake them in the oven.

To cook

Rub the chestnuts through a sieve. Slowly fold in the stiffly whipped cream and the sour cherries. Fill the fried pastry with this mixture. Dredge with confectioner's sugar.

Chestnut horns

Printed in Hungary, 1987
Kner Printing House, Békéscsaba
CO 2522-h-8789